HOW GREEN ARE YOUR WELLIES?

Annie Tempest

MULLER, BLOND & WHITE

First published in Great Britain in 1985 by Muller, Blond & White
55 Great Ormond Street, London WC1N 3HZ

Reprinted 1985
Copyright © 1985 Annie Tempest

British Library Cataloguing in Publication Data

Tempest, Annie
How green are your wellies?
I. Title
741.5′942   PN6737.T4

ISBN 0 584 11126 6

The caption on page 50 is taken from *How To Get On
In Society* by John Betjeman (*Collected Poems*) which is
reproduced by kind permission of John Murray
(Publishers) Ltd.
The illustration on page 40 is partly dedicated to
Adam Posing-Pouch M.B.O. (Muscle Bound Oaf)

Printed and bound in Great Britain by
R.J. Acford Chichester

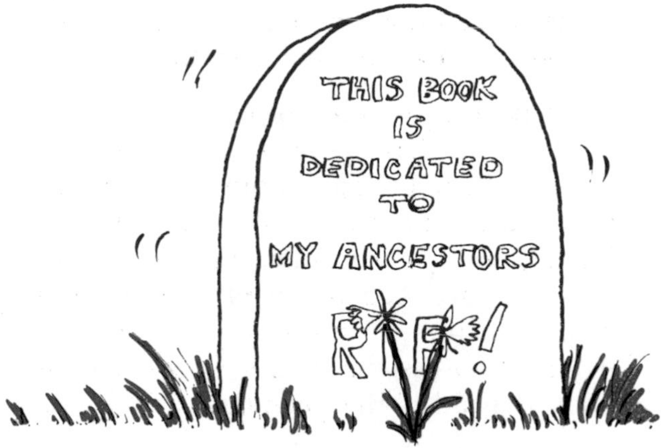
THIS BOOK
IS
DEDICATED
TO
MY ANCESTORS
RIP!

FOREWORD

The Green Welly, in keeping with other English institutions, has a family tree. Commissioned by the Duke of Wellington as an accessory for the Cavalrymen it long remained popular as a riding boot. Indeed, its connection with the horse has lingered on. Today's customised Green Welly has a buckle to remind us all of its noble forebears. The Welly itself has become an emblem of the haughty-culture where once all it had to do was to keep water out. Many a hooray wades in from the wine and cheese belt to Threadneedle Street unconcerned about the drought.

Annie Tempest chronicles this eccentricity. She is a keen observer of a disappearing tribe, but her attention has also been drawn to an *appearing* one. The past five years have seen an unprecedented adoption of the county plumage by the Gucci set aided by manuals. Annie's cartoons fight back. She lampoons Lavinias draped in Laura Ashley (one wallpaper pattern fits all) and pigsticks Fionas festooned in horse-tackle motifs. She likes her hoorays but wants to keep them English - unsullied by wop designer labels. She also wants to man the barricades against incursions in the country world led by the Harpie and Queen Yorkie-Barr media set. All these obsessions are documented within. This is not so much a 'how-to-do-it' guide but the book that takes the peerage out of Burke's.

In Wellis latexis plodamus

Do you have any four-poster cots?

Nice bunny rabbit.

Gervaise is joining Jardines, but for Rupert it'll have to be Knight, Frank & Rutley.

Oh you'll ADORE India, I did it in March.

I say, you MUST try a Beedee.

But can one have a coming-out party from a closet?

Mama, meet Lady Augusta Fortnums-Queue-Smythe-Tempest-Fitzwallop-Highlandwhoop
– Tits for short.

I believe the red ribbon means she kicks.

Maximilian has always been the black welly of the family.

There's always SOMEONE more interesting than me.

Tell me, what do YOU do?

How FAScinating – I'd always assumed
'a stiffy' was a smart invitation.

I'd like to take your daughter to Paris on approval for the weekend.

Looks like a game bird.

Certainly got a fine brace.

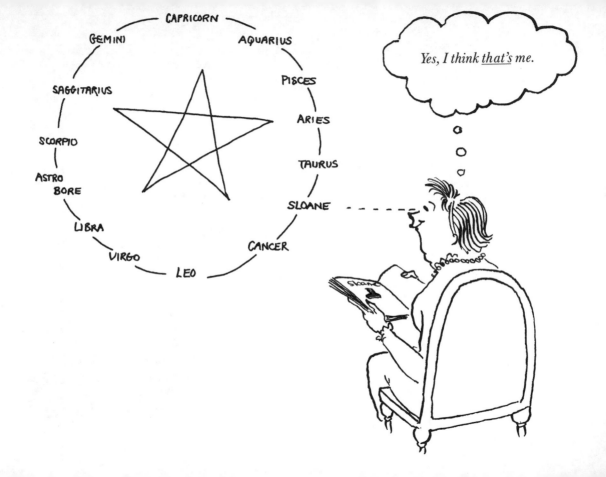

For Lent I'm giving up hope of hooking a husband before I'm 25.

You with your inheritance, I with my crumbling stately home . . .

Oh do look Plip-Plop, there's Screetch, Fungus, Filth, Sniffer and Squawk.

This is my fourteenth time.

HENRIETTA

*M.B.O.**   *SHALLY OISEAU*

Yuk! Hairy wellies.

I'm afraid I've lorst the ice bucket.

Let me just check if I've got your number in my address book.

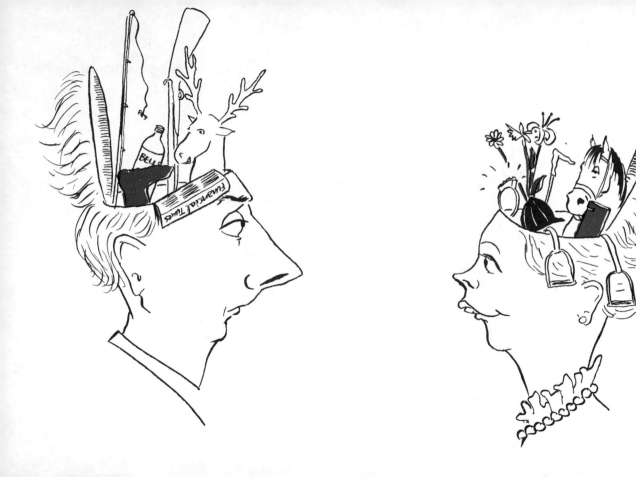

I think I've realised my creative destiny.

"Phone for the fish knives, Norman."

I'd like one of those nice pointed aristocratic schnozzles and if you could remove my chin and make my teeth protrude just a little . . .

Daddy insisted when we became nouveaux pauvres.

I shay! Shtop those damn stairs, I want to get on.

He was HIDeously disobedient when I got him.

But Daddy he's in <u>gold</u>.

As a member of the upper class, Henry, I suggest you stop being so middle class and get 'em orf.

His Lordship's a vegetarian.

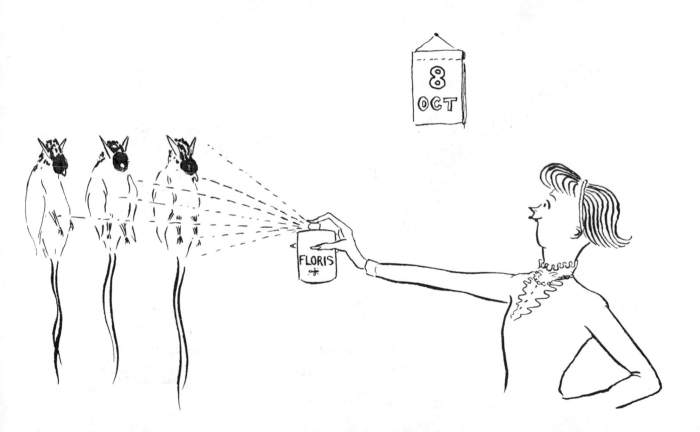

Your amaryllis cuttings or your life!

We'll have to get down wind of this one.

Of course I knew him when he was only plain Lord Legge-Ferret.

BUST
OF
THE EARL OF VOLE-TROWSER

We don't give a damn if it's a boy or a girl, providing its ears stick out.

OLD SCHOOL TIE

Cordelia, where are you?

Doctor says it's an overdose of Laura Ashley.

Talk about a mixed marriage – there's Father Levi talking to Bishop Montefiore.

I too am an immigrant. My family came to England with William the Conqueror.

This one's going to be a designer husky – I'm using pink thread.

Come on darling, we can't possibly let them down at the last fence.

Bang goes our chance of an invite to Clarence House.

OK, OK a joke's a joke
– it's not as if I chose it.

There are times Charles when tits beat titles hands down.

This looks as good a place as any to pitch marquee.

What won't the deaf old fossil be able to hear?

*Extraordinary really, that yawn reminds me
of a crocodile I shot while serving in the
QDG in '59.*

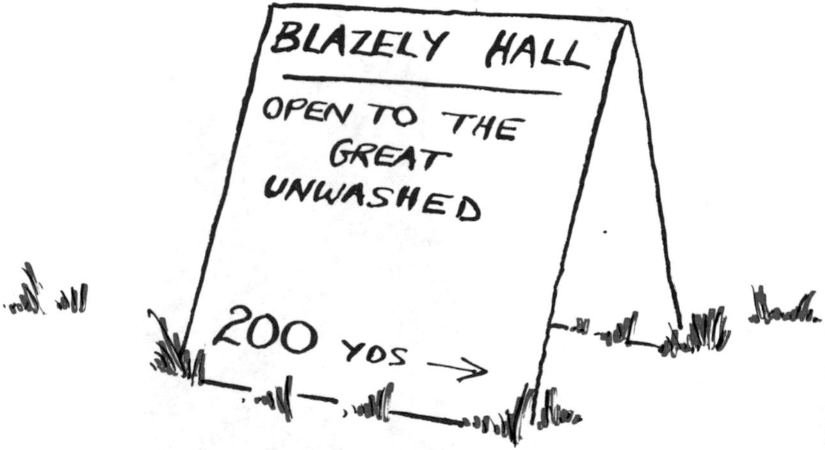
BLAZELY HALL
OPEN TO THE GREAT UNWASHED
200 YDS →

Arthur, are you SURE it's not a Bank Holiday?

I do love a nice cosy TV supper.

It had better be good coke.

I'm afraid the butler died 50 years ago.

Only another quarter of a mile to go.

. . . and here under the portrait of the present Duke and Duchess is the only radiator in the house.

Bring the C5 to the smoking room would you, Norman?

Do you Charlotte Albertine Elspeth take Edward Wathen Courtney Torquill . . .